#DigitalPD for Educators

Dr. Matthew Woods

Dr. Sam Fecich

ABOUT THE AUTHORS

DR. MATTHEW WOODS

Education Administrator, CEO of Leading Out the Woods LLC, Host of the K-12 Podcast: Leading Out the Woods.

DR. SAMANTHA FECICH

Associate Professor of Education, Author of EduMagic: A Guide for Preservice Teachers, Host of the Podcast EduMagic Future Teacher.

HEY TEACHER, YOU GOT THIS!

As a new teacher, you must ensure that your professional development is aligned with your teaching philosophy. In this book, you will learn strategies, techniques, and tips to help you succeed in your first year as a teacher.

TABLE OF CONTENTS

GETTING STARTED

Why do I need to own my PD?

As teachers, we know that learning doesn't stop when we cross that stage at graduation - it is just beginning. We must stay informed about best practices, changing educational technology, and standards. That is why you need to be able to select your professional development path.

OK, but I'm getting PD from my school, isn't that enough?

The school district will provide you with district-level professional development, which will be scheduled and delivered by the district. Your school district usually hosts a day of professional development for the entire school. This is one type of professional development model. Teachers can usually benefit from this model, although it is only tailored to some. The school or district requires us to attend professional development events.

In some cases, the information gained from such events can be practically applied in the classroom. In other cases, they may not be relevant to our classroom or learners, but we must sit through them.

We will not discuss the PD model provided by your district expressly. Instead, we will focus on choosing your adventure model of professional development. This flexible model allows you to learn how you learn best and where you would like to grow as an educator.

Because of this, this model is flexible and can be adapted to fit your learning style and pace. As a result, professional development can be arranged according to your schedule. This is our preferred method of professional development, where you get to choose your PD. It is so easy to develop our Professional Development when there are so many resources available to us.

Notes

Think about what areas you would like to strengthen this year. What are some areas where you would like to make improvements?

Notes

HOW & WHY IS SOCIAL MEDIA IMPORTANT?

When we refer to "social media," we refer to Merriam-Webster's definition: electronic communication (such as social networking websites and microblogging) through which people can share information, ideas, personalized messages, and other content (such as videos). Does this definition align with what you wrote down? Where did you find discrepancies that caused you to have a different interpretation?

With its authentic (and intended) representation, social media is a valuable resource to modern society. Its ability to benefit and support people wherever they are is one of the main reasons why it continues to grow. It bridges the communication and outreach divide that has persisted throughout human history. Sir Francis Bacon, the founder of the Royal Society, once proclaimed, "Knowledge is power." He was right. Before innovative communication and networking tools, knowledge was siloed in different communities and groups. In recent years, social media has allowed individuals to share ideas and network with others across the country and around the world.

Additionally, discussing ideas can lead to people becoming curious. Before we had high-speed Wi-Fi connectivity and prolonged dial-up internet (how many of us remember how long it took to refresh new emails in our inboxes?), we gained our collective knowledge in these ways:

1. Going to the library to review books, magazines, articles, journals, and micro-films.
2. Get firsthand information from your teachers, mentors, and family members.
3. Life experiences.

The internet has made all three of these vitally important, but social media allows quick access through its hodgepodge nature. People have become more curious and creative thanks to this development.

How about hopping on Google to quickly search for a random thought? Want to improve your home but need to figure out your ability to do it yourself? For a quick tutorial, check out YouTube. Digital technology has accelerated the process of gaining foundational knowledge.

So, what kind of learning techniques do you find most enjoyable? Are you a fan of listening to content? How about watching videos? Do you attend in-person events? Are you interested in reading articles? Post your ideas below.

Let's put these two ideas together and see how they blend! Exercises like this can be repeated year after year or semester after semester. By reflecting on areas where you shine and grow, you can create a plan to improve those areas. Reflecting early on in your career will help you more than you can imagine! Make this an interactive process!

You will discover how social media and the consumption and creation of media can provide you with opportunities for professional development. It's time to get started!

While we have wonderful colleagues down the hall from us in our various buildings, social media allows us to reach out to other teachers in our grade level, subject areas, administrators, and leaders from around the world. Just a click of a button can connect us with so many brilliant minds.

In social media, educators can share ideas, be encouraged, and learn from one another.

Create a list of ideas you are curious about regarding your instruction or curriculum using the template on the next page. For example, you might incorporate visuals into your daily bell ringers to engage students or help transition between groups and individual assignments.

PROFESSIONAL DEVELOPMENT WITH SOCIAL MEDIA

Ok, but do I need accounts on every platform?

Short answer: (drumroll) NO. Were you surprised to see that? Well, you can be on some platforms posting daily. Having a presence on every platform every day is optional. Instead, find a social media platform (or two) that you can visit and interact with regularly as a teacher.

In addition, we encourage you to consider different platforms from an educator's perspective - YES, even Instagram! Try them out for about one month to experience the benefits of social media accounts. Keep the ones you enjoy and delete those you don't engage with as much. However, give yourself time to connect, share, and learn on social media.

A broad range of social interactions has been affected by social media over the past fifteen years. What began as a way for individuals to stay connected has grown into countless other forms of communication. Before diving too deeply into the topic, let's establish what the term means. Using your prior knowledge, write out the definition you think of when you hear "social media."

Notes

WHY DO WE NEED ACCOUNTS?

Now that you've learned what social media is and what it can do, it's time to explore the various accounts you can access. Our social media world is expanding daily with new apps, websites, or combinations. Although it may seem overwhelming, the variety of choices makes it more likely that you will find something that appeals to you.

We could have inflated this educational processing guide to 100+ pages with all the different accounts available, but that wasn't our intention. Instead, we want you to understand the importance of social media to professional development. Using this approach, we will guide you through some ways to begin your learning and growth.

You must become familiar with and comfortable creating social media accounts to accomplish this. Depending on your age and generation, you probably already have at least one personal social media account.

As an educator, you are often held to a high standard (often blurring the line of being unrealistic). Remember to keep in mind that social media creates a digital catalog of everything you post and communicate. Let's break it down further: everything you post, like, comment on, reply to, share, or repost represents YOU!

In this processing guide, we will examine the following social media platforms: Facebook, Twitter, Instagram, Podcasts, Pinterest, and digital portfolios (which will include references to items such as LinkedIn, OneDrive, and Google Sites). As we stated, we intend to refrain from promoting one form over another.

Instead, we will provide you with an overview of the many options available to help you expand your professional knowledge. Review the Social Media Account Checklist before diving into the different sections about these items. Consider what information you will enter in these sections as your accounts develop. There might be slight differences in terminology when setting up the apps on each platform, but they all follow this generalization.

SOCIAL MEDIA ACCOUNT CHECKLIST

STEP 1

What's in a username?

Select a username that is as close to your real name as possible and consistent across all your social media accounts. Don't be afraid to be creative.

STEP 2

Picture

Upload a photo of just you! Your photos don't need to be glamour shots, but professional and with a bit of personality! Ensure people can find you on your social media accounts using the same picture.

STEP 3

Writing your bio

A bio should be professional, purposeful, and personal. Be sure to add your personality to your teaching story. If you are interested in a particular field of study, consider including hashtags in your bio. Be clear and share who you are as a person and an educator.

STEP 4

Links!

Use a single link on your social media accounts. It can be a link to your digital portfolio or where people can learn more about you.

STEP 5

Add some glitter

We can't add glitter to our accounts, but we can customize colors and header images and add emojis to our bios. Create an account that reflects you!

AS YOU CREATE YOUR CONTENT, SHARE IT OUT ON YOUR SOCIAL MEDIA NETWORKS WITH #DIGITALPDFOREDUCATORS

LEARNING ON SOCIAL MEDIA

Notes

Take a moment to reflect on what you have learned so far. What are you particularly interested in learning more about? Do you have any ideas for posts?

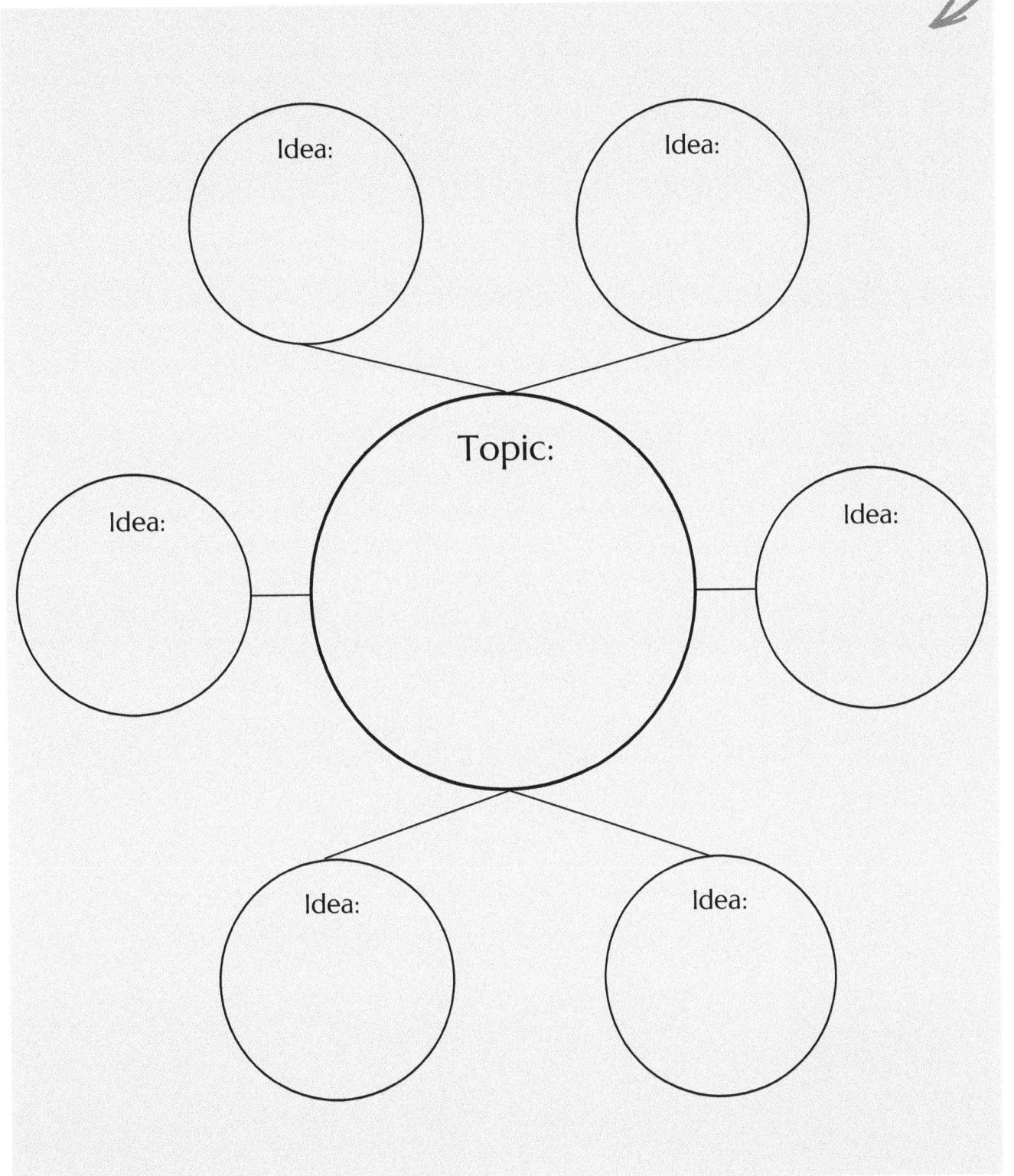

10 Commandments of Smart Social Media

Michael Fertik (April 30, 2014) outlined the Ten Commandments of Smart Social Media that we believe also apply to educators. We added a bit to them too.

- It is essential to understand that privacy settings will only partially protect you. Make sure you read the privacy settings for each account you create. So, it would be best if you were mindful of your post.

- Don't post during raw emotion - reflect on what you post and why. Think about the purpose of the post - is it meant to engage, educate, inspire, and motivate?

- Turn the digital cheek to posts that offend. We all know that song We Didn't Start the Fire by Billy Joel, so don't fan the flames or be a flame thrower. If someone posts something or replies/comments in a way you disapprove of, you can delete the comment, block it, or unfollow it.

- Check out who you are following, what they are posting, and who they are following. Consider why you follow the people you do. Be mindful about who you follow. Don't follow someone just because they follow you.

- Never share racist, sexist, or crude content and then express surprise at the professional and personal fallout. You are a professional - act like it in all facets of your life.

Notes

10 Commandments of Smart Social Media

Michael Fertik (April 30, 2014) outlined the ten Commandments of Smart social media that also apply to educators.

- Don't forget that strangers' eyes may always be drawn to thy posts. Post and comment with integrity each step of the way.

- Your actions online are judged by others, just as you judge them. If you're going out with friends or having a fun night, keep this in mind when you post about it.

- Check your accounts to see who is following you and who is following you. As a professional educator, you should manage your accounts accordingly.

- Whenever you post on social media, remember that you are a professional. As an educator, you are being looked at by others through that lens. Think about what you post and how it may come across to others.

- Social media isn't as important as personal interactions. Remember to connect in real life. Be mindful of your relationships.

Notes

https://www.inc.com/michael-fertik/10-commandments-smart-social-media.html

AFTER CREATING YOUR ACCOUNTS

So, you've created your accounts. Now what? It's simple, let's learn first. While some professionals refer to this as lurking, we prefer to call it learning. Two reasons: first, it's not creepy, and second, as teachers, we're always learning and growing, and social media is a beautiful way to do so. You can learn much by seeing what others do on social media in their classrooms.

Customize your feed to reflect your professional image. Feed your teaching soul by following accounts that challenge, and inspire you, no matter where you are in your career or what you hope to accomplish. To build a quality Professional Learning Network (PLN), you should follow educational leaders and see who and whom they follow. Hint: feel free to follow the authors' social media accounts listed at the beginning and end of the book as starters.

Second, look for hashtags related to your grade level, content area, subject area, certification, or interests in the field of Education.

Post what you've learned and are doing - the more voices, the better. Social media is a wonderful place to share your positive, professional self.

Notes

CONNECTING WITH TWITTER

Twitter allows you to send short messages to others via your cell phone or computer (or 'Tweet'). Undoubtedly, Twitter has contributed to the need for concise communication in many ways. Initially, Twitter had a character limit of 140 characters before increasing it to 280 characters. Many of us are already familiar with short message service (SMS) platforms from text messaging.

Today, people of all ages want information as quickly and efficiently as possible. Twitter receives your tweet and sends it to its servers. People who have either 'followed' you (that is, found your username and added you) or found your tweet because of the hashtags you have included will receive this.

You choose whom to follow based on your interests and what you want to gain from the platform. You can see a person's tweets and other items on their profile when you follow them on Twitter. In the search bar, you can either find a tweet you like or search for a person's username. To follow either one, click the 'Follow' button at the top of the page.

Identify educators on Twitter with whom you would like to connect by making a list of your favorite hashtags and terms. Get a feel for a potential Tweet by using the Twitter Template before posting it.

Notes

SOCIAL MEDIA PITFALLS

Below are a few recommendations for interacting with students on social media. To ensure compliance, you must first determine the social media policies of your school and district. Many districts refrain from posting pictures of students or providing personal information about them on social media. Some teachers put an emoji face over pictures of their students when posting them online. Even if the post is positive, please protect the children's identities. Please send a note to families explaining how you plan to use social media and asking them to sign off on the permissions.

Some school districts prohibit educators from using social media to interact with students, even for educational purposes (i.e., following a student's Twitter account or creating a Facebook class page). It would be best if you spoke with your school district's respective building principal and communication department to ensure that you do not unintentionally do anything inappropriate. Before posting on social media, seeking guidance is a good idea.

Make sure you are familiar with the social media policies of your school or district.

Notes

CONNECTING WITH TWITTER

The Twitter Template directions are as follows:

1. Draft some tweets using the corresponding template.
2. Remember that you only have up to 280 characters (including all letters, characters, and spaces in your post).
3. Remember to include #hashtags to help others find them.

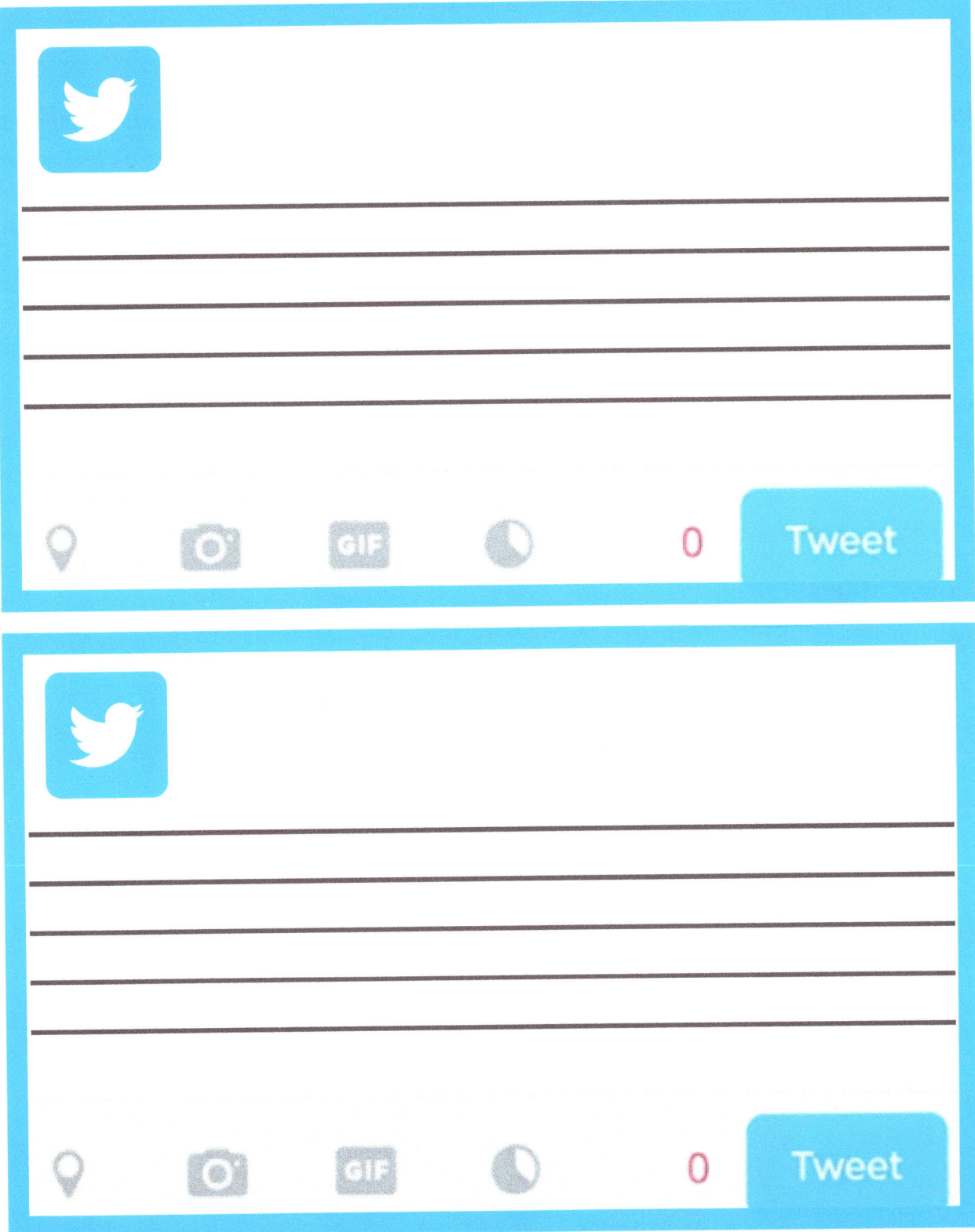

AS YOU CREATE YOUR CONTENT, SHARE IT OUT ON YOUR SOCIAL MEDIA NETWORKS WITH #DIGITALPDFOREDUCATORS

CONNECTING WITH TWITTER

Twitter Strategy?

Having described Twitter briefly, let's get to the fun part! Here are some activities to help you get more comfortable using Twitter for your professional development. Regardless of your social media, it would be best if you were consistent. You can start by posting three times per week. You can use the following simple strategy:

Monday - Learn about a topic that interests you in Education. Use this day to search Twitter for ideas, strategies, and techniques.	**Tuesday - Ask a question to the community using related hashtags, images, or gifs.**	**Wednesday -Share a resource you created with images or links and hashtags related to the topic.**
Thursday - Shout out a favorite resource such as a blog, journal, podcast, or online seminar.	**Friday - Shout out to two people that you learned from this week.**	**Saturday - Search for a new way to teach something.**
Sunday - Take a break!		

Notes

CONNECTING WITH TWITTER

Class Twitter Chat Activity

A Twitter Chat is an excellent way to get students (and even parents/guardians) talking about a topic in a virtual space. Although it appears cumbersome initially, this activity is an excellent means of leading and generating discussion. Usually, Twitter Chats last between half an hour and an hour at a scheduled time.

Participants search for and respond to questions and answers posted using preselected hashtags. Before using a hashtag for your chat, please make sure it has been vetted. You can do this by searching the hashtag you have in mind and seeing if others have used it and if they have posted something unrelated to your topic.

Here are a few articles to help you get started with Twitter chats:

- https://www.teachbetter.com/blog/getting-started-with-twitter-chats-for-teachers/
- https://www.iste.org/explore/professional-development/44-education-twitter-chats-worth-your-time
- https://www.sfecich.com/post/how-to-slay-your-first-twitter-chat
- https://www.edutopia.org/blog/introduction-twitter-education-chats-robert-ward

You can participate in Twitter chats at any time if you bookmark this site at http://sites.google.com/site/twittereducationchats/education-chat-calendar. Please keep in mind the time zone in which it is listed and frequently updated with active and inactive listings. Also, if you want to attend one of the Twitter chats listed, please double-check the hashtag an hour or so before the chat to make sure it is still on. For instance, if the chat is scheduled for 7:00 PM, you can check Twitter around 6:50 PM to see if anyone has tweeted about the chat. If so, participate in the chat; if not, the chat may have been canceled or rescheduled. Look for another one to attend and learn from. This site may be less up-to-date, but it is the most comprehensive, and educators often refer to it.

Before the Twitter Chat, the moderators post the questions at predetermined times. Some may also have a set time when they post answers, while others post questions and respond to responses as they see fit. Usually, responses result in multiple conversations and micro conversations on various threads related to the questions. Sometimes the most exciting conversations happen during side conversations. You can go ahead and skim through and comment to see how participants responded. It is optional to answer every question posted in a Twitter chat. The following template can be used as a guide when creating your Twitter chat.

CONNECTING WITH TWITTER

Please follow these guidelines when posting your Twitter chat activity:

Answer 1 (A1) compose your response to question one. Your response should include the chat hashtag. You should also include A1 so participants know which question you are responding to. You should also post the answer within about four minutes of the question being asked.

The topic of the Twitter Chat:
The hashtag for Twitter Chat: #

- Time:
- Question 1 (Q1)
- Answer (A1)

- Time:
- Question 2 (Q2)
- Answer 2 (A2)

- Time:
- Question 3 (Q3)
- Answer 3 (A3)

- Time:
- Question 4 (Q4)
- Answer 4 (A4)

- Time:
- Question 5 (Q5)
- Answer 5 (A5)

CONNECTING WITH TWITTER

You might find it helpful to make some cards with the same information that you can post on the Tweet after you have drafted the questions and answers. One of the recent Twitter Chats hosted by Dr. Woods moderated for #aussieED is shown below.

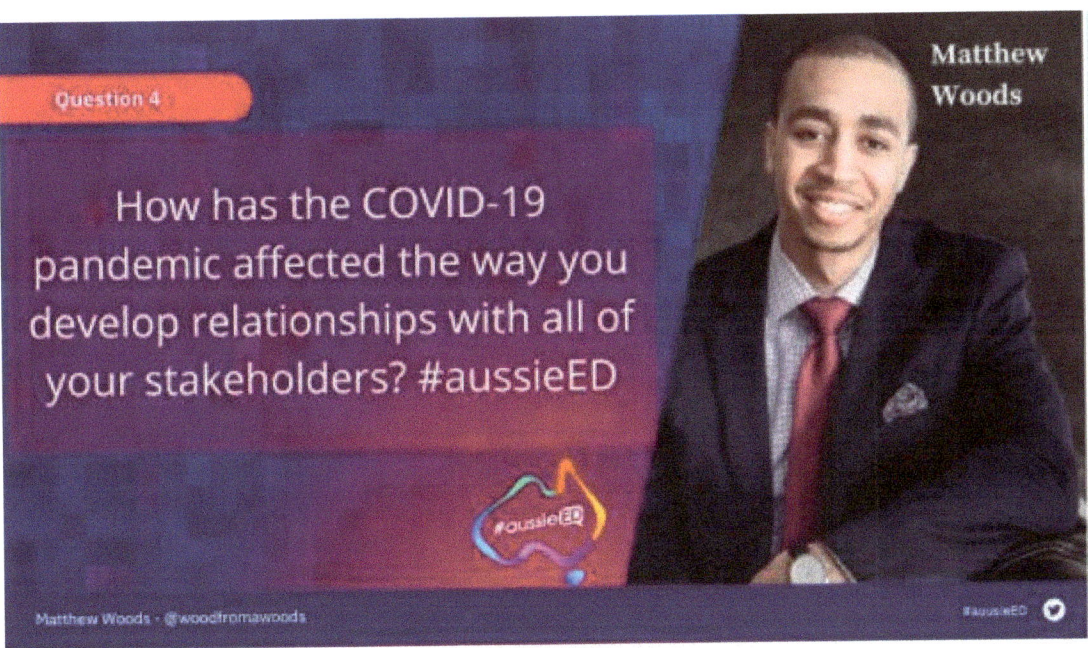

You can easily create these graphics with Canva for EDU or Buncee. Your card should include the following:
- Question number
- Question prompt
- The hashtag for the chat
- Moderator handle

CONNECTING ON TWITTER

Let's take a moment to consider what we have learned about Twitter so far. Have you reviewed the Twitter Chat calendar? Are there any Twitter Chats you'd like to attend?

Notes

...ugh Instagram, educators, future educators, school districts, and ...nizations can connect and learn from each other. You can learn a ...y reading posts, stories, lives, DMs, reels, and guides.

...e are the ways you can connect on Instagram:

Posts: are pictures or graphics that contain text information. ...onsider posting something educational three times a week as a ...eacher. Teachers can be inspired by images that show what they ...are doing. Here's an example from @chrisemdin: ...https://www.instagram.com/p/CdPH7QLMo-E? ...utm_source=ig_web_copy_link.

Stories: is a picture or video that lasts only for 24 hours. Choose an ...icon above your following usernames on your home page.

Lives: Video sessions hosted by one, two, three, or four people. You ...can listen, participate in the conversation, and learn from others ...during these live sessions. They are sometimes posted in feeds, so ...you can tune in later if you miss them live.

DMs (direct messages) are private messages sent between two ...people. Groups of private messages can also be created. You can ...share text, images, emojis, and voice memos in these messages. ...This is a wonderful way to connect on a more one-to-one basis.

Reels: Share 90-second clips of video. The videos are meant to be ...quick and impactful. Use this resource to share a quick tip, a ...teaching strategy, or a teaching tool. Check out this example posted ...by @michaelbonner_: ...https://www.instagram.com/reel/COQ9zRVhjla/? ...utm_source=ig_web_copy_link

Guides: Digital leaflets with content and links. Using these ...resources, you can create a guide for different teaching grades and ...content areas.

CONNECTING WITH INSTAGRAM

This is an excellent way to brainstorm ideas for your teacher's Instagram account. Use the Big 3 Bucket method to keep your Instagram feed interesting to other viewers and impactful to you. Identify three topics that are meaningful to you as a teacher and that you are passionate about. In special education, buckets might include accommodations, assistive technology, adapted activities, or organizing tips for IEPs / paperwork.

Teacher education, educational technology, and advice for future teachers are three areas of interest for Dr. Sam. You can brainstorm different ideas and organize them into subcategories. For instance, in IEP tips, you can give an example of a SMART IEP goal. You can meet more educators and share content by having differentiated feeds tailored to your interests and passions. You won't have to think of something to post every day or the same thing every day.

Notes

CONNECTING WITH INSTAGRAM

Notes

In the space below, identify your three big and smaller buckets.

Bucket 1 Topic	
3 areas to share about in bucket 1	
Bucket 2 Topic	
3 areas to share about in bucket 2	
Bucket 3 Topic	
3 areas to share about in bucket 3	

CONNECTING WITH INSTAGRAM

Instagram recently announced plans to become a video platform. There are many ways to share video content on Instagram, including Lives, IG TV, Reels, and Stories. Post a video once a week on Instagram using one of these features. These features allow you to create and share video content on Instagram.

Here are some tips to help you think through video content on Instagram:
- Do's and Don'ts in your field.
- Five favorite tools or ideas for the topic area
- Five common misconceptions
- Your grade level's top educational books.
- What is your favorite edtech tool for the classroom?
- Share about your favorite classroom resources and materials.
- A technique or strategy you tried and how it went in the classroom.
- Share a favorite podcast, book, or article you are reading to show an experiment.
- Host an IG Live with an expert in the field or the author of a book you read.

IDEAS TO POST ON INSTAGRAM

This is an excellent way to brainstorm ideas for your teacher's Instagram account.

Notes

CONNECTING WITH INSTAGRAM

Below are two examples of Instagram posts Matthew has created. One post talks about a podcast episode. The other refers to his online mini-series course. As you can see, the post included the following: a visual, a description, and hashtags. The hashtags make his posts appear when other educators search for similar posts on Instagram, expanding his reach and audience.

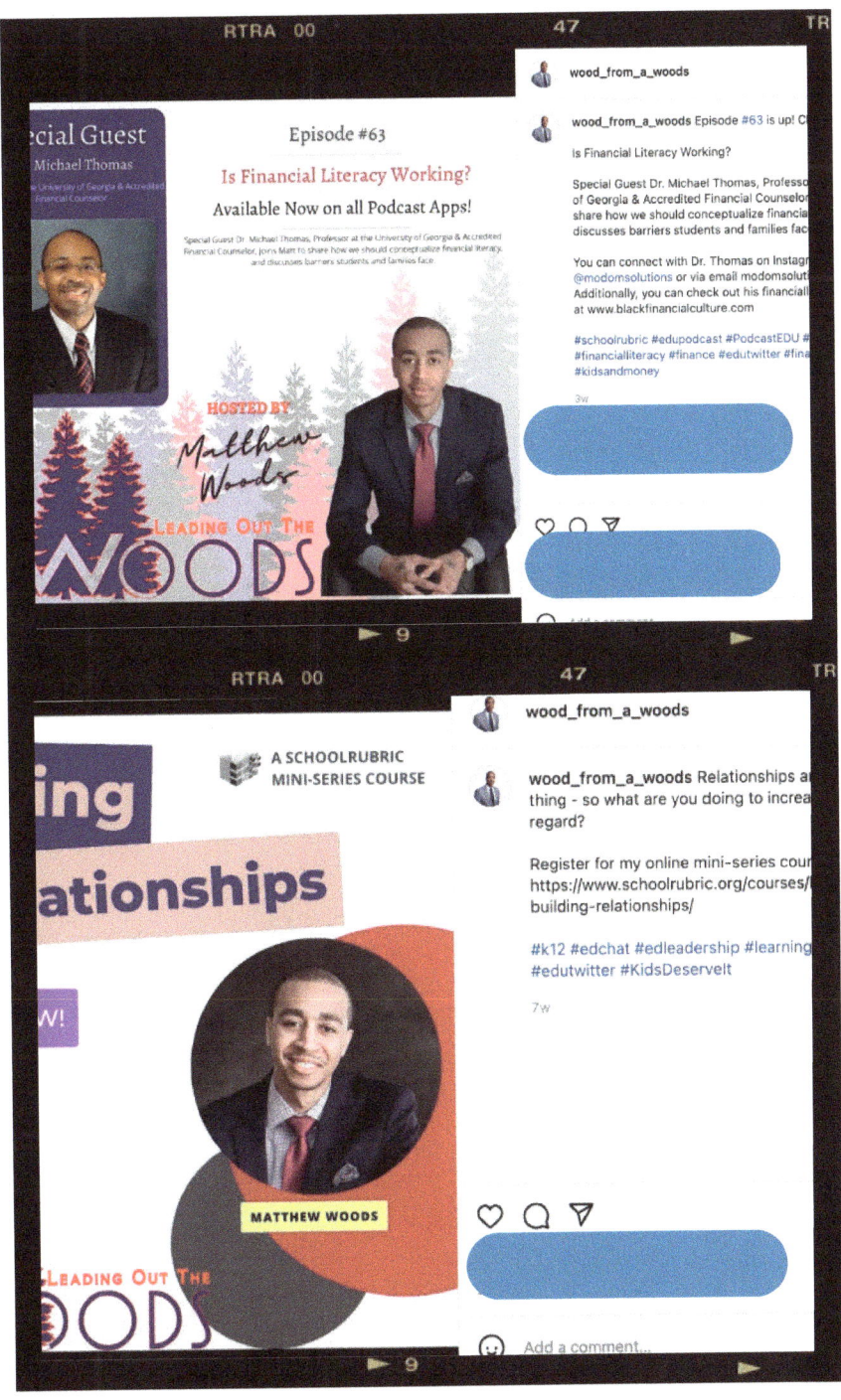

01

Quote

Share a motivational quote, song lyric, or verse that speaks to your teaching heart. Using Canva, create a quote graphic and explain why it is essential to you in the caption.

02

How to

We all have our way of doing things. Share your favorite teaching how-to strategy with your audience. Tell us one of the strategies, manipulatives, or resources you used to instruct your students. Please add a video!

03

Resources

Share your favorite resources for back to school, a specific topic, formative assessment, family communication, etc.

04

Carousel

Create an image carousel that shows how something is done or your steps in a process.

05

Go LIVE!

You can share a technique, pedagogy, or method you tried this week live with your followers. Reflect on your learning - be authentic and share what's in your heart.

06

Share a story

You can share your day-to-day happenings here! Additionally, stickers and polls are great ways to engage people.

CONNECTING WITH FACEBOOK

Harvard students created Facebook (or Facemash as it was then known) to judge other students' attractiveness. Despite initially being shut down for violating university policies, its creators quickly realized how successful an online social network could be based on the response from their peers. In February 2004, it was renamed TheFacebook.com. Through this free website, peers (who signed up) could share information about themselves with others.

Examples include class schedules, photos with friends, and other information about their lives. As a result, other colleges and universities began signing up to be a part of this growing online platform. Different companies and other interested parties reached out to advertise their products. Facebook is regarded as the first online social network to leverage direct engagement between advertisers and consumers.

The Newsfeed displays various news from Facebook, such as upcoming events, posts, changes to friends' profiles, advertisements, etc. Typically, this is where people review what their connections share regularly. When members scroll through the Newsfeed, they see various posts—the only information shared by your friends and people you choose to follow displayed, except for advertisements. Over two billion people use Facebook monthly, which means that the News Feed option has considerable influence over what information is disseminated and digested.

A Profile is created when you want to share personal things (such as family pictures and random inspirational quotes) while storing all your website information. Unless you publicize your posts (and other information), only people you have added as 'Friends' may view them. Prepare a list of information you would like to include in your profile.

Notes

CONNECTING WITH FACEBOOK

Page: Like a Profile, a Page is a business account representing an organization or company. It would help if you first had a Profile to create a Page. You can then create and link as many pages as you want from that Profile. You can also 'follow' others by liking the page, and their News Feed (like Twitter) will display your updates. In a structured online environment, you can also use it to share information with your parents and students. There is also a feature called Insights, where the page will provide you with information about who viewed your content, how they interacted with it, and other valuable analyses.

Group: A Group extends the concept of a Page by allowing a business or organization to promote various activities. These groups help generate conversations around several topics and allow followers to start these conversations themselves if they choose. It would help if you also remembered that a Group could be public or private, depending on how it is set up. We highly recommend using the Facebook professional development feature over the other two to engage in online professional development. This keeps your personal information safe because you can create a separate, professional-only Group. Furthermore, members can begin leading discussions on diverse topics once the group is set up with the premise.

Stories: This content lasts for 24 hours. Stories consist of pictures and videos that play for a brief period. You can either share them with your 'friends' or send them directly to them via messenger. When you and your friends post a Story, it will appear in the Newsfeed at the top of the page. The post will appear when you select it.

Facebook Messenger: The messages are personal, one-to-one, from users to each other. Facebook Messenger is a separate, accompanying app that allows users to message in addition to the website. When attempting to send a message through Facebook, you will be prompted to download an add-on/different application on your mobile device or web browser. In addition to sending messages, you can also make voice and video calls, start group chats, and add emojis to regular conversations.

Notes

CONNECTING WITH FACEBOOK

Below are a few ways you can use Facebook in your daily instruction to engage your students:

Profiles of Historical Figures

This is an excellent way to differentiate students' fact-finding or biography assignments. Rather than students taking notes, you could have them create a Facebook profile for a historical figure. Since the Profile would be 'fake,' we recommend providing students with a template that they can use to input their findings. Although they aren't doing this online, they still need to create a profile page for their Facebook account. You can find many templates online to use. Below is a free example we found on Teachers Pay Teachers by Kari Mosbacker. You can also find a similar activity on ClassTools.Net called "Fakebook."

Use a classroom Facebook Page to post resources, communicate information to students and families, and track the level of engagement. Think about how often you send mass emails to all students, and I hope they all read them. You can use Facebook analytics to determine how many students and families have interacted with posts and assignments on your page.

*Before doing this, you must review your district's policies before engaging with students and families on social media.

Create a Poll

A Facebook poll is one way to gather input from students. Polls can be differentiated based on various factors. An example of this (but not limited to):

- Feedback about the upcoming topic in class
- Pre-assessing students' prior knowledge about a topic
- Formative assessment of an assignment

This strategy could be a follow-up to the classroom page since students must be members of the page before they can access it.

Follow these simple steps to set yourself up and get started:

Step #1. On the Facebook Home Screen, find and click on your Page tab.
Step #2. Select the Publishing Tools tab.
Step #3. Select Create Post.
Step #4. Click on the ellipsis (they look like three dots), then choose poll.
Step #5. Type the Question you want to ask, and for Option 1 and Option 2, enter the options for your poll. Add more if needed depending on the topic.
Step #6. Underneath the Poll Options, click on the "1 week" drop-down to choose when you want your poll to end (for example, one day, one week, Custom).
Step #7. Click on the Share Now button.

Notes

CONNECTING ON FACEBOOK

Let's take a moment to reflect on what we have learned about Facebook. What are some groups you might be interested in? As a professional educator, what are some pages you may want to interact with?

Notes

LEARNING FROM PODCASTS

Podcasts are audio shows covering a wide range of topics. You can listen to podcasts on almost any topic you can imagine. Podcasts last between ten minutes and one hour (or longer). You can subscribe to podcasts for free. Podcasts can be listened to on Google Play, Apple, Spotify, iHeartRadio, Pocketcast, and TuneIn. With these apps, you can subscribe to shows, get new episodes automatically downloaded, and interact with show notes, guests, and hosts. This PD model is easy and convenient to use if you are in the community, doing chores around the house, going for a walk, or exercising. Learning while doing something else is a great option.

Everyone can access podcast episodes and shows. Make sure you subscribe and listen! You're sure to enjoy them. Check out our recommendations on the next page if you're looking for a few shows. Try opening your favorite podcast player and searching for teacher podcasts and shows. Episodes will appear on your player. Also, you can use resources like those below to help you search.

There is a podcast network of podcasts for teachers created by teachers at http://www.edupodcastnetwork.com/. From future teachers to administrators and everything in between, you will find a little of everything here!

Articles about podcast recommendations for teachers:

- https://www.weareteachers.com/must-listen-podcasts/
- https://blog.edpuzzle.com/teaching-today/the-best-teacher-podcasts/
- https://blog.feedspot.com/teacher_podcasts/
- https://www.edutopia.org/article/13-educator-approved-podcasts-listen-year

Notes

LEARNING FROM PODCASTS

EduMagic, hosted by Dr. Sam Fecich. This podcast is for preservice teachers. Dr. Sam Fecich interviews preservice teachers as she discusses how EduMagic is helping them achieve their educational goals.

Leading Out the Woods, K-12 podcast hosted by Dr. Matthew Woods. Dr. Woods reflects on experiences & best practices working in K-12 Education as a former teacher & current administrator. Additionally, he invites various educators from across the country as guests for discussions. New episodes are released bi-weekly on Fridays at 4 PM (excluding special bonus episodes).

House of Edtech hosted by Chris Nesi. Learn about educational technology and how to use it in the classroom with a purpose and meaning. Give Chris' tagline a try - educational technology isn't difficult.

10-minute Teacher podcast hosted by Vicki Davis. This show will leave you with all the teaching feels - inspired, encouraged, and driven to do better for my students. Check it out; each day has a different theme, and they're all great.

Teachers on Fire podcast hosted by Tim Cavey. Three words to describe this podcast - inspiring, motivating, and engaging. In his interviews, he looks at how significant changes in Education are changing the educational landscape.

The Counter Narrative is hosted by Charles Williams. It is a podcast dedicated to changing how Education is discussed and viewed. Even though the field is far from perfect, plenty of impressive work is done daily.

The Teaching Tales podcast is hosted by Brent Coley. This podcast will capture your imagination and inspire your passion for teaching. Brent recently published a book called EduInfluence for more inspiration.

TeacherCast, is hosted by Jeff Bradbury. This show gives people tips on starting their podcasts for professional development or sharing with students.

YOUR FAVORITE SHOWS:

LEARNING FROM PODCASTS

Now that you have read a few ways you could utilize podcasts to encourage individual and group professional development list some other ways you could see it being used.

Notes

LEARNING FROM PODCASTS

Two Strategies for using Podcasts in your PD:

Below are a few of the ways we have seen podcasts used to support individual and group professional development for educators. We encourage you to try them out! This first is called Reflection Journals. This is one of the most popular ways teachers can use podcasts in professional development. After listening to a podcast related to a topic of interest, the teacher writes a small reflection and turns it into their supervisor if you are still trying to figure out what and how this could look over the example below.

Scenario to Consider

Summer just finished her pre-evaluation with her principal, Deborah, and both concluded that Summer should focus on her inclusion and delivery of formative assessments in her daily instruction to monitor student behavior. Her principal provides a few resources to help get her going (two books related to formative assessments, and pairs her with a veteran teacher (thought partner) known for implementing high-quality formative assessments. Deborah encourages her to think about other strategies she feels would be appropriate and follow up with her next week. The following morning, while going on her daily jog and shuffling through music, Summer stumbles across the podcast, Leading Out the Woods, Episode #23, Quick Jabs: powerful, succinct Formative Assessments featuring Allison Zmuda. After listening to the episode, Summer jotted some notes down about what she learned and shared them with Deborah on Monday. Her principal loved the idea and told her to take out the books she had given her last week. To Summer's surprise, one of the books was titled Students at the Center: Personalized Learning and Habits of Mind, co-authored by Ms. Zmuda.

Consider this layout for documentation of a podcast for professional development purposes:

Title of Podcast: Episode title:

Link:

List three bright ideas gained from the show:

How do you plan to implement what you learned from the episode?

LEARNING FROM PODCASTS

Podcasts are fantastic learning opportunities for learning on the go. We decided to work on a piece for you to reflect upon your learning when listening to podcasts.

Notes

TITLE OF PODCAST:

EPISODE TITLE:

LINK:

LIST 3 BRIGHT IDEAS GAINED FROM THE SHOW:

HOW DO YOU PLAN TO IMPLEMENT WHAT YOU LEARNED FROM THE EPISODE?

AS YOU CREATE YOUR CONTENT, SHARE IT OUT ON YOUR SOCIAL MEDIA NETWORKS WITH #DIGITALPDFOREDUCATORS

LEARNING FROM PODCASTS

Another strategy to use podcasting for professional development would be to consider the following question. How many of us have attended professional development conferences and meetings where the presenter takes the first portion to provide the context of the problem to the audience?

While understanding the 'WHY' behind whatever you discuss is highly helpful, imagine if that information was front-loaded to colleagues to save valuable time. Podcasts are great ways to get folks to think about the topic and give them a solid frame of reference before you begin your meeting. Check out the example below for a way to utilize this strategy.

Scenario to Consider

Curtis has been teaching for seven years and is highly respected within his school for his teaching and continued professionalism. Curtis's principal, Lori, has asked him to assume the role of Mentor Teacher Supervisor this school year. The primary duties consist of assisting Lori in pairing up mentors with newbie teachers (anyone with three years or fewer of experience) for support, monitoring the frequency of their weekly check-ins, and setting up monthly meetings to cover different topics as grading practices and assessments. While heading to the teacher's lounge to make copies of his syllabus for back-to-school night, Curtis overhears several colleagues talking about how they are not looking forward to 'wasting' thirty minutes or so in the initial mentor meeting.

Curtis goes to Lori and asks her if it is okay if he sends out a few reflection questions related to the podcast, EduMagic: Future Teacher Podcast, which is a podcast designed for preservice teachers. Lori approves, and Curtis asks them to listen to episode #112, Tips from a new teacher mentor featuring Michelle Randall, and reflect on the accompanying questions before their meeting to shave off time for the upcoming meeting. A few days later, Lori and Curtis are heading down to the workroom to begin the meeting with the mentors and newbies. To their shock, many are already having conversations and working through items. When Curtis asks what's going on, a colleague replies: "We listened to that show you sent us, and it gave us ideas on what we need to elaborate with newbies when we meet with them."

LEARNING FROM PODCASTS

Consider this layout for documentation of a podcast for professional development purposes:

What are topics that are on the professional development plan for your school?

Is there a list of speakers coming to your school?

What episodes of shows can you listen to that feature the topic or the speaker?

LEARNING WITH PINTEREST

Our favorite tool for searching, collecting, and curating content is Pinterest. I used Pinterest for recipes and crafts when it first came out. I just realized how powerful Pinterest is for the classroom. Pinterest is a visual search engine, not a social media platform like Twitter and Instagram. You can think of Pinterest as a visual version of Google. This mindset shift is helpful when you start using Pinterest in your classroom. The site is a space for searching topics, including strategies, ideas, and how-tos.

If you are looking for new, fresh ideas for your classroom, Pinterest is a beautiful place to look. It is made up of boards, pins, and stories. Using Pinterest, students and teachers can create a board for content related to their classes, grade level, subject area, certification, professional development, and lesson plans.

You can find inspiration and information on Pinterest by searching for ideas. Create a Pinterest account and start collecting and curating content just for you. Then, you can display, collect, and curate content tailored just to you with your own Pinterest account. It is easy to fall into the comparison trap with so many ideas - meaning just because a teacher is doing something in their classroom does not mean you should copy them. Because only YOU know your students, you must do what is best for them.

Features:
- Pins - items that are saved to your board.
- Board - Collection of pins.
- Idea pins: Content that lasts for 24 hours.

Notes

LEARNING FROM PINTEREST

We love that Pinterest can be customized to meet your needs and goals as a teacher. A public or private board can be created, even one that is collaborative! Get those ideas flowing! What are some boards you would like to see on your Pinterest account?

Are you looking for more resources to help you get started with Pinterest? Check out: https://www.sfecich.com/post/pinterest-to-connect-and-learn.

Notes

_____
_____
_____
_____
_____
_____
_____
_____
_____
_____
_____
_____
_____
_____
_____
_____
_____
_____

LEARNING FROM VIDEO CONTENT

Video content is a great way to learn and grow as an educator. Videos can provide you with an inside look at tutorials, how-to's, tips, and resources. Video content can cover many fields, which is an overly broad concept. In general, what is most important to remember about video content is that it provides visuals and models of whatever is being discussed. Conveying innovative ideas to people unfamiliar with the subject can be highly effective. More than 40% of people prefer watching visuals rather than reading text. For most occupations today, training tutorials include brief video clips demonstrating and explaining the proper techniques.

VIDEO OPTIONS

- YouTube
- Vimeo
- Webinars live
- Webinars recorded or archived
- Virtual summits
- TikTok
- Stories on Facebook
- Stories and Reels on Instagram
- Idea Pins on Pinterest

In this processing guide, we have included some of the most common ways video content is used in educational settings.

As teachers read various excerpts in class, they can incorporate video clips that visualize what was already prepared and branch off from what was just discussed. Differentiating your instructional delivery while keeping students engaged is a great idea.

Notes

LEARNING FROM VIDEO

With online conferences and webinars now being hosted via video, it's possible to learn a great deal with video content. Make a list of any live, recorded, or archived webinars you are interested in attending.

Notes

Try searching YouTube for educational content, topics, etc. Make a list of educational YouTube channels you should subscribe to.

Notes

Set notifications for those accounts that inspire and motivate you on social media so you never miss a video post, reel, or IG Live.

Notes

LEARNING FROM VIDEO

Scenario to Consider

Raphael has been paired with incoming novice teachers for several years as a mentor. In this capacity, Raphael shares instructional strategies, "words of wisdom," and other advice pulled from his 15+ years of experience in the classroom. One of the most impactful tools he has found is having them observe several lessons throughout the school year. At the end of those days, Raphael pulls them together to debrief and give his mentees a chance to ask clarifying questions about their observations. While setting up his classroom for back-to-school night, Assistant Principal Camile drops by his classroom to chat. "Hey Raph, I know you are busy getting set up for tonight, but I want to give you a heads up on the revised schedule that was tweaked.

Due to the anticipated substitute (teacher) shortage and duty assignments, we won't be able to have the mentees observe your classroom for the first several months." While Raph is visibly disheartened, he understands. As Camile is getting ready to leave, he has an idea. "What about having them watch me on the Swivl? I could record my lessons and then share them after school. They could watch them by a set date, and we can all meet to discuss." Camile likes the idea a lot, and thanks, Raph, for the suggestion. That school year, Raph and his administrators began successfully using that strategy. Eventually, other teachers and colleagues adopt it to learn from each other's instruction.

Notes

LEARNING FROM VIDEO CONTENT

Video content

As you teach a new concept, you can get mixed reactions from students, from smiles and nods showing that they understand to confused looks. You might also get students who come to class late or are absent for that period. It is a problem we all face, and you always try to get caught up as fast as possible. Alternatively, you can record your lessons and direct instruction portions so your students can access them on your teacher's webpage or another way. It lets your students rewatch anything they're still unsure of and ensures they hear the same message.

Observing others:
Technology such as iPads, Swivels, cameras, and other recording devices allow teachers to observe their colleagues in action. Suddenly, there are many opportunities for learning that we were previously unable to take advantage of. Consider observing your colleague in another school across the district or even across the country. Before these various innovations, you were restricted by your school. Your ability to learn from others has now been extended.

Self-Reflection:
The average person becomes defensive when given feedback from someone else. One way to chip away at that barrier is to critique yourself first by watching yourself teach. I know that for me, watching myself is extremely difficult. I often think, "Do I say 'um' that many times while I am speaking with someone?" and "Why do I slouch instead of standing straight up when speaking?" Like many of you, we, indeed, are our own worst critics. However, at the same time, we are more accepting of our flaws when we see them with our own eyes.

Notes

VIDEO CONTENT TOOLS

Here are a few tech tools to help you create video content. The tools selected below are easy to use, free (for the most part), and fun to use! Check out a few and get started creating video content today.

Flip - This tool helps with deliberation or having students demonstrate what they know in different ways. Flipgrid lets students record their screens, record audio, or record video. Dr. Sam Fecich has used this tool with her students as an introduction activity. This tool helps students get to know one another before class begins, helping them make connections and recognize faces.

Other ideas for Flipgrid include:
- Book reviews
- Social-Emotional Learning activities
- Introductions for class
- Presenting content
- Reflecting on assignments or assessments

You can create some of the content yourself when presenting it! Students can assist in creating video content. For example, in Dr. Sam's class, she has students create an ignite presentation using Flipgrid about each of the 22 Danielson Framework for Teaching Components. Students should watch each video to gain a better understanding of the components.

Screencastify or Loom - You can install these browser extensions to create 5-minute videos. You can record your screen or talk on video. You can then share the video links.

Canva EDU and PowerPoint recording - Use these tools to create video presentations with your slides and video in the corner of the screen. This tool is excellent for creating and sharing information about an issue, topic, strategy, or content.

Notes

DOCUMENT YOUR LEARNING

The journey toward learning never ends. Make sure that you are documenting your progress! In this digital age that we live (and teach in), capturing the fantastic things your students do in their classrooms with current technology is crucial. It's still possible to lug binders full of artifacts with you. However, when everything is stored in a digital catalog, you can display it whenever you need it. Below are a few ideas to get you started:

LinkedIn: This is a great space to share your work milestones, professional accomplishments, awards, and resources. This tool is a beautiful space to connect with other professionals in the education space. Like Facebook, it allows members to create profiles and connect with others online. The main difference between the two is that LinkedIn targets professional criteria for potential connections, such as job industry and titles. At the same time, Facebook uses your interests to make these potential matches.

Strategies for using LinkedIn: One of the most obvious ways is to collaborate with other professionals online. Like other websites mentioned in this guide, LinkedIn is set up to connect like-minded professionals in a shared space for growth and networking opportunities. One of the many ways we have found this beneficial is by connecting with colleagues after a conference or professional development online seminar. Instead of swapping email addresses and phone numbers (which you are happy to do still), you can 'add' them on the platform to continue the conversation. Additionally, you can see their professional portfolio (such as job experience, places they have worked, complementary skills, etc.) and get a better feel for them.

Another great strategy is to join an existing professional group on LinkedIn. Joining professional groups like Social Studies Education, Science Teacher, and New Teacher lets you connect with other like-minded professionals looking for support and interaction. Additionally, you can ask different questions, share topics, and participate in a variety of discussions that take place.

Notes

DOCUMENT YOUR LEARNING

Flash Drive: Flash Drives are small data storage devices that contain information. They can easily fit into your pocket to take with you to copy some of the information you gain from a conference or house the artifacts you will present at the next grade-level meeting. Flash Drives are also great ways to hold bootable versions or various operating systems for your desktop or laptop. A flash drive is another valuable resource if you can't access the internet. Hey, it's happened to all of us.

Online storage such as OneDrive, Dropbox, or Google Drive. These storage options are fantastic because your content lives online in the cloud. You can access this content across devices. You can also share content through viewing or editing permissions provided to colleagues and team members.

Notes

DOCUMENT YOUR LEARNING

You can also create a digital portfolio to document your learning. You can create a digital portfolio that you can update, edit, and add to as you see fit using free online tools like Google Sites, Wix, WordPress, and Weebly.

- Creating a digital portfolio is an effective way to highlight your awesomeness.
- Welcome - is the first page visitors see when they land on your site. You introduce your digital portfolio and explain its purpose to viewers.
- About me - The about me page lets you get more personal with your content. Include information about who you are outside of teaching: your professional resume minus any personal contact info.
- Contact: The contact page is self-explanatory. Include your professional email, embed, or provide a link to your social media feed. Please don't include your address or phone number– there are creepers.
- Work samples - student work samples (removing identifiable indicators), lesson plans, materials, and resources used in the class.
- Letters of recommendation
- Professional development blog: Keep track of your PD in a blog format.

Resources to get started:
- https://www.sfecich.com/post/digital-portfolios-the-place-for-all-of-your-eduawesomeness
- https://www.sfecich.com/post/3-steps-to-digital-portfolio-success-featuring-amanda-jeane-richert
- https://www.sfecich.com/post/time-to-brush-the-dust-off-that-digital-portfolio
- https://www.sfecich.com/post/5-things-most-teacher-candidates-do-wrong-when-setting-up-their-digital-portfolio

THANK YOU!

We hope this processing guide inspired you to grow and learn as an educator in new ways. Teachers are lifelong learners - they continue to learn if they are teaching.

To continue your learning journey with us, check out our resources.

CONTACT THE AUTHORS

DR. MATTHEW WOODS

Education Administrator, CEO of Leading Out the Woods LLC, Host of the K-12 Podcast: Leading Out the Woods.

DR. SAMANTHA FECICH

Associate Professor of Education, Author of EduMagic: A Guide for Preservice Teachers, Host of the Podcast EduMagic
Future Teacher.

AS YOU CREATE YOUR CONTENT, SHARE IT OUT ON YOUR SOCIAL MEDIA NETWORKS WITH #DIGITALPDFOREDUCATORS

REFERENCES

Bacon, F. (1597). Meditationes sacrae.

Fecich, S. (Host). (2021, February 11). Tips from a new teacher mentor featuring Michelle Randall [EduMagic: Future Teacher Podcast]. https://podcasts.apple.com/us/podcast/tips-from-a-new-teacher-mentor-featuring-michelle/id1462923850?i=1000508630275

Fertik, M. (2014). The 10 Commandments of Smart Social Media. Inc. https://www.inc.com/michael-fertik/10-commandments-smart-social-media.html

Joel, B. (1989). We Didn't Start the Fire [Song recorded by Billy Joel]. On Storm Front. Columbia.

Mosbacker, K. (2012). Facebook Template (Handout). Teachers Pay Teachers. https://www.teacherspayteachers.com/Product/Facebook-Template-Handout-260839?st=d240abbf314d6fc5d66f4b35c821606c

Social media. (2021). In Merriam-Webster.com. Retrieved December 9, 2021, from https://www.merriam-webster.com/dictionary/social%20media

Woods, M. (Host). (2021, January 15). Quick Jabs: Powerful, Succinct Formative Assessments featuring Allison Zmuda [Leading Out The Woods]. https://podcasts.apple.com/fr/podcast/quick-jabs-powerful-succinct-formative-assessments/id1507447161?i=1000505441085